THE PASSOVER JOURNEY

THE PASSOVER JOURNEY
A SEDER COMPANION

by BARBARA DIAMOND GOLDIN

illustrated by NEIL WALDMAN

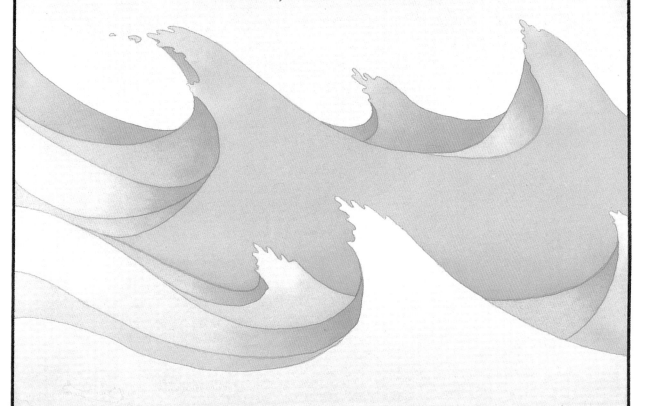

PUFFIN BOOKS

Special thanks to Dr. Barry W. Holtz, codirector, Melton Research Center, Jewish Theological Seminary of America; Judith Herschlag Muffs, director of special projects, Anti-Defamation League; Professor David G. Roskies of the Jewish Theological Seminary, who all read this text for background authenticity.

Please note: Part One intermingles Biblical texts with Midrash (rabbinic stories and commentaries). For more information, see "Notes on Sources."

PUFFIN BOOKS
Published by the Penguin Group
Penguin Books USA Inc., 375 Hudson Street, New York, New York 10014, U.S.A.
Penguin Books Ltd, 27 Wrights Lane, London W8 5TZ, England
Penguin Books Australia Ltd, Ringwood, Victoria, Australia
Penguin Books Canada Ltd, 10 Alcorn Avenue, Toronto, Ontario, Canada M4V 3B2
Penguin Books (N.Z.) Ltd, 182-190 Wairau Road, Auckland 10, New Zealand

Penguin Books Ltd, Registered Offices: Harmondsworth, Middlesex, England

First published in the United States of America by Viking, a division of Penguin Books USA Inc., 1994
Published in Puffin Books, 1997

10 9 8 7 6 5 4 3 2 1

THE LIBRARY OF CONGRESS HAS CATALOGED THE VIKING EDITION AS FOLLOWS:

Goldin, Barbara Diamond. The Passover journey : a Seder companion / by Barbara Diamond Goldin;
illustrated by Neil Waldman.   p.   cm.
Includes bibliographical references.
Summary: Retells the story of the Israelites' fight for liberation from slavery in Egypt
and explains the traditions of the Passover Seder.
ISBN 0-670-82421-6
1. Passover—Juvenile literature. 2. Seder—Juvenile literature. [1. Passover. 2. Seder. 3. Exodus, The.
4. Jews—History—To 1200 B.C.] I. Waldman, Neil, ill. II. Title.
BM695.P3G58 1994 269.4'37—dc20 93–5133 CIP AC

Puffin Books ISBN 0-14-056131-5

Printed in the United States of America

CONTENTS

PART ONE

The Israelites' Journey: The Story of the Exodus

THE NEW PHARAOH

Ancient Egypt was a sunbaked land of golden sand and endless stretches of desert. It was also a land of lush green fields and palm trees that flourished on the banks of the life-giving river, the Nile, which ran like a ribbon through the thirsty desert.

It was into this Egypt that the Israelites settled thousands of years ago, when there was a great famine in Canaan, their own land.

They were welcomed by the godlike ruler of Egypt, the pharaoh, and by his people, even though they were different. For the Israelites had their own language and religion.

The Israelites worked as shepherds on the land for many years. They multiplied and they prospered.

Then a new pharaoh came to the throne, one who was distrustful and unmerciful. He was afraid of the Israelites because they were different. He said that in time of war, they would join the enemy and fight against Pharaoh and his people.

This new pharaoh made the Israelites into slaves. He hoped they would grow weak working in the broiling Egyptian sun. He hoped they would bear fewer children. He hoped they would grow sickly and die.

Making bricks and mortar and building cities under the cruel watch of Pharaoh's taskmasters became the Israelites' lot instead of shepherding their own flocks. The taskmasters whipped them, beat them, sometimes even killed them.

More straw. More bricks. Higher walls. Pharaoh increased the slaves' burdens. With all this, the Israelites still had sturdy, healthy babies. They still grew in numbers. And Pharaoh was still afraid of the Israelites.

His magicians' prophecy played on his fears. "One day a boy will be born to the Israelites," they said. "He will grow to be their leader and free them all from slavery."

Pharaoh could not rest. He ordered the midwives, Shiphrah and Puah, who ministered to the Israelite women, to kill each newborn Israelite boy.

The good women could not bear to follow Pharaoh's orders. They gave him excuses, saying, "Those Israelite women are so strong. They give birth by themselves, before we even arrive."

So Pharaoh thought of another plan. He ordered that all baby boys born to the Israelites must be thrown into the waters of the Nile River.

What sorrow and anguish filled the hearts of the Israelites when they learned of Pharaoh's newest command.

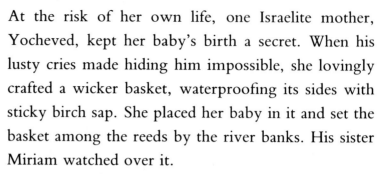

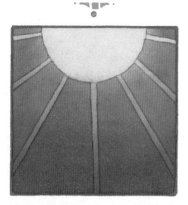

BABY MOSES

At the risk of her own life, one Israelite mother, Yocheved, kept her baby's birth a secret. When his lusty cries made hiding him impossible, she lovingly crafted a wicker basket, waterproofing its sides with sticky birch sap. She placed her baby in it and set the basket among the reeds by the river banks. His sister Miriam watched over it.

Boats sailed down the river, but only birds came near the basket. Then Miriam heard splashing in the water. She saw that Pharaoh's daughter had come to bathe.

Pharaoh's daughter noticed the basket. "Fetch it," she told a slave girl.

Pharaoh's daughter opened the basket and saw Yocheved's baby. She knew he was an Israelite and pitied him, for she was not as cruel as her father.

Miriam saw the princess's face soften with love, and stepped forward.

"I know a Hebrew woman who could nurse the baby for you," Miriam bravely told the princess. "Shall I get her?"

"Yes," said the princess.

So Miriam ran and brought the baby's own mother, Yocheved, back to Pharaoh's daughter.

"Nurse this child for me," the princess said. "And I will pay you."

Feelings of joy and hope overwhelmed Yocheved, but outwardly she was calm and serious and agreed to the princess's command.

MOSES GROWS UP

Yocheved kept her son for three years. Then, as had been agreed, she brought him to the princess, who took him as her own.

"I'll name him Moses," the princess said, "which means, 'I drew him out of the water.' "

This is how Moses, an Israelite, came to grow up in Pharaoh's palace.

Though Pharaoh could be a cruel ruler, at home in his palace he would sometimes play with the child Moses and laugh at his games.

One day, while Moses sat on Pharaoh's lap, he reached for something pretty and glittery that Pharaoh was wearing. It was his crown. Moses took the crown and playfully put it on his own head, giggling as he did so.

Pharaoh did not think this was amusing.

"Look how the boy took my crown!" Pharaoh said indignantly to his advisers. "Maybe this Israelite that my daughter drew from the water wishes to take away my kingdom. I have not forgotten the magicians' prophecy."

Pharaoh and his advisers decided to test little Moses

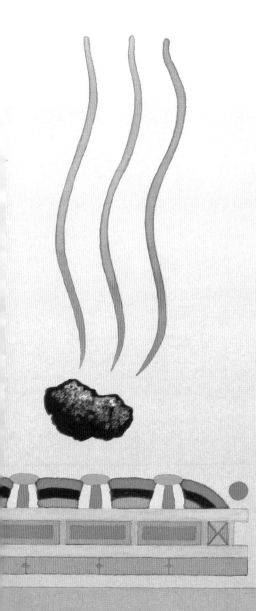

by putting two objects in front of him, a glowing piece of hot coal and a shiny piece of gold.

"If he takes the hot coal," said one of the advisers, "then we know he was just being playful and meant no harm to you. But if he reaches for the gold, then we know he is greedy and cunning and may someday take away your kingdom."

The coal and the gold were put before little Moses. When the child began to reach for the gold, God sent the angel Gabriel to help Moses. Gabriel pushed Moses' hand away from the gold, so that Moses grabbed the coal instead.

As a child often does with shining objects, Moses put the hot coal into his mouth. He immediately cried and dropped the coal, but it was too late. The coal had burned part of his lips and tongue. From then on Moses spoke with a stutter, but at least he was saved from Pharaoh's anger.

Even though Moses grew up in the comfort of Pharaoh's palace, he did not forget his brothers and sisters, the Israelite slaves. He would watch them make mud bricks and carry them from one place to another. He helped them with their burdens whenever he could, for it pained him to see how they were being treated.

One day he saw a slave master severely beating a slave. This so outraged Moses that he stepped in, struck the Egyptian, and killed him.

Afterward, Moses grew afraid of what would happen to him if Pharaoh learned what he had done, so Moses ran away to the land of Midian.

GOD CALLS TO MOSES

In Midian, Moses worked as a shepherd for the priest Jethro and married one of his daughters, Zipporah. They had two sons, Gershom and Eliezer.

While Moses was in Midian, the pharaoh of Egypt died, and a new one took his place. The Israelites worked harder than before and cried out to God for help. God noticed them and God noticed Moses.

One day, when Moses drove his flock of sheep into the wilderness, he saw a thorn bush and stopped. The bush was burning, but nothing burned around it.

Slowly, Moses moved closer. He could see that though the bush was on fire, its leaves and branches were not burned by the flames.

"How can this be?" Moses said. He stared at the bush, for he had never seen such a fire.

Then he heard a voice from inside the bush call, "Moses! Moses!"

Moses looked around. There was no one. He looked at the bush and answered, "Here I am."

God spoke from within the bush. "I hear the cries of My people in Egypt. I will send you to free them from slavery, to bring them to a land flowing with milk and honey."

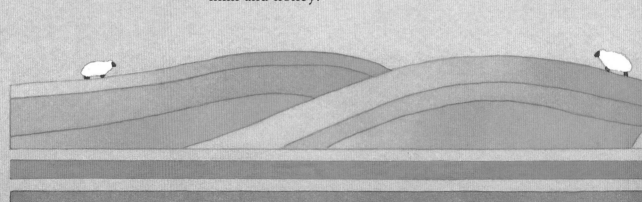

"Me? Go before Pharaoh?" protested Moses. "The Israelites won't believe that I was sent by You to bring them out of Egypt. Nor will Pharaoh."

"I will give you some signs," said God. "Throw your rod on the ground."

Moses did this and the rod became a snake, slithering before him on the ground.

Then Moses put his hand under his clothes, as God commanded, and when he removed it, the skin on his hand was ugly and scaly. He hid his hand once again, and it became like the rest of his body.

"If Pharaoh is not convinced by these signs, then take some water from the Nile River and pour it on dry ground. The water will turn to blood," God said. "Tell Pharaoh to let My people go. Warn him of the signs and wonders I will bring upon Egypt."

"But what about my stutter?" Moses said, still afraid.

"There is your brother Aaron," said God. "He speaks well and he will help you. Even now, he is coming to meet you. Go back to Egypt, Moses. I will be with you."

MOSES AND AARON SPEAK TO PHARAOH

When they came to Egypt, Moses and Aaron spoke with the elders of the Israelites. They showed them and all the Israelites God's signs. The people recognized God's presence and rejoiced.

Then Moses and Aaron went to see the pharaoh.

When they appeared before the palace guards, Moses and Aaron seemed different from other men and awed the guards. They stood as tall as cedar trees. Their faces shone like the sun, their eyes radiant like the morning star. When they spoke, their words jumped from their mouths like flames. The guards let Moses and Aaron enter the palace without a question.

But Pharaoh had questions.

"Who are you?" the ruler of all Egypt asked. Moses had so changed since his days in the palace that Pharaoh did not recognize him.

"We are messengers of God," answered Moses and Aaron. "And God says, 'Let My people go!' "

"Who is this God, and why should I listen to what your God says?" Pharaoh responded angrily.

"The One God's strength and power fill the world," Moses and Aaron answered. "God stretched out the earth with a word and created the mountains and valleys. All living things and spirits, God has made."

"I do not know God," Pharaoh said. "The names of the gods of all the nations are written in my records. I do not find your God written anywhere."

"Your books have the names of statues, of idols," said Moses and Aaron. "The One God is a living God."

"A lie!" shouted Pharaoh. "I am the master of the world. I created myself and the Nile River that sustains us."

Not only did Pharaoh refuse to let the Israelites go and pray to God, he increased their work.

"Let them gather their own straw to make bricks," he told the slave masters. "But tell them this. They must still make the same number of bricks as before."

The Israelites complained to Moses. "Since you came, things are worse for us."

Moses spoke to God.

"You will reassure the people with My promises," God said. "And I *will* bring the Israelites out of Egypt. But I will send signs and wonders first, so all the Egyptians and Pharaoh will know that God is working among them."

THE TEN PLAGUES

Moses and Aaron went before Pharaoh again. They told Pharaoh that if he did not let the Israelites go, God would work signs and wonders in Egypt.

"God will turn the waters of the Nile to blood," they said.

"My magicians can do this trick," Pharaoh boasted. "Why should I let the Israelites go?"

So Aaron stretched his rod over the waters of Egypt and God sent the first sign. All the water in this hot, dry land turned to blood, even in the wells and drinking cups. All except the water in the land of Goshen, where the Israelites lived.

Moses and Aaron went before Pharaoh. "God says, 'Let My people go or I will send a second sign and plague your whole land with frogs.' "

Pharaoh would not listen.

So Aaron stretched his rod over the waters, and a giant frog appeared. As he walked, armies of little frogs leapt from the giant frog's mouth. Down the road they

went, into the Egyptians' homes, into their beds, ovens, and bread bowls. The frogs were everywhere, under and over and in between.

"Stop these frogs!" Pharaoh said. "And I will let your people go."

As soon as the frogs were gone, Pharaoh became stubborn again.

So God sent a third sign to Egypt. When Aaron struck the dust of the earth with his rod, every particle of dust turned to lice. The tiny insects lodged in the Egyptians' hair and nested on their animals. All of Egypt itched and scratched.

Pharaoh's own magicians said: "Our spells cannot produce lice. This is God's work." But Pharaoh would not listen to them.

God sent a fourth sign to Egypt. Out of the desert came lions, panthers, scorpions, and snakes, racing, leaping, biting. Birds of prey circled through the air, darkening the light of the sun and the moon.

"Go," Pharaoh said. "Take your people. Just ask God to remove these creatures."

God sent the wild animals back into the desert, and Pharaoh changed his mind.

"God says, 'Let My people go or there will be more signs and wonders in Egypt,'" Moses told Pharaoh.

But Pharaoh remained stubborn and would not let the Israelites go.

God sent more signs to Egypt. A fifth. A sixth. A seventh. The animals of the Egyptians—their horses and donkeys, camels, cattle, and sheep—became sick and died. Boils and blisters fell onto the Egyptians, covering their bodies with sores and pain. And a fiery hail fell on the land, striking all that were in the open field—man, animal, grass, and tree.

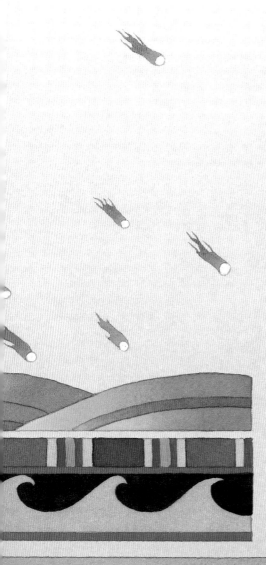

As soon as one plague stopped, the Pharaoh would break his word and refuse to let the Israelites go. God would work another sign on the land.

An eighth. A ninth.

Locusts came and the whirring sound of the thousand thousands of their wings filled the land. These insects ate every bit of green left after the hail, every leaf and every blade of grass. They filled the palaces and houses of the rich and the poor.

Then a darkness settled over Egypt, so thick that the people could touch it and feel it. They were frightened of it. Never had the Egyptians seen such a darkness before. They couldn't move from their places nor see another person or animal, even if they were next to them.

Then God told Moses about the tenth and most terrible plague.

"After this sign," God told Moses, "Pharaoh will let My people go. To keep the Israelites safe, they must listen and do these things that I tell you.

"You must take a lamb and slaughter it. Then you must dip a leafy branch in its blood and mark your doorposts with this blood as a sign to Me.

"You must roast and eat the lamb with unleavened bread and bitter herbs. You must eat hurriedly with your sandals on your feet, your staff in hand, ready for what this night will bring. Do not go outside the doors of your houses until morning.

"You are to remember what happens this night and celebrate it throughout the ages."

The Israelites did everything that God told Moses they should do. They sacrificed and ate, watched and listened.

In the middle of that night of waiting, the Israelites heard a terrible wailing come from the houses of the Egyptians. The firstborn of the Egyptians were dead— male and female, the servants' and Pharaoh's. But the Israelites were safe, for God had seen the blood on their doors and *passed over* their houses.

Pharaoh went looking for Moses in the night. Being a firstborn, he was afraid that he too would die. He hurried to Goshen, where the Israelites lived, calling for Moses as he wandered through the streets.

Moses and his family were inside their house eating the roast lamb and singing praises to God.

"Moses," Pharaoh begged at the window when he had found the right house, "what can I do to end this plague?"

"Call out, 'Israelites, go free,'" said Moses. "Call loudly."

Pharaoh called out. Miraculously, his words were magnified so that the call to freedom sounded throughout the land of Egypt.

THE ISRAELITES LEAVE EGYPT

The Israelites—hundreds of thousands of them—hurried out of Egypt on foot, before Pharaoh changed his mind. They followed Moses and Aaron with their flocks of goats, donkeys, cows, and sheep, carrying their food, their kneading bowls wrapped in clothes upon their shoulders. The unleavened cakes on their backs baked into flat, crispy bread as they walked toward the desert under the bright Egyptian sun.

Slaves so long, they were suddenly free.

To guide them on their journey, God went before the Israelites. By day God moved in a pillar of cloud, by night in a pillar of fire. In this way, the people walked away from Egypt.

But Pharaoh did change his mind. When the Israelites reached the Sea of Reeds (also called the Red Sea), they could hear and see Pharaoh's chariots and horsemen chasing after them.

They called out to Moses. "Look! The Egyptians come from behind us! And the sea is in front of us!"

"We would rather serve the Egyptians than die here in the wilderness!"

"Don't be afraid," said Moses. "God told me to hold my rod above the sea so it will split open for us."

Moses held his rod over the waters of the sea. "Go forward," he told the people.

Despite Moses' words, the people were still afraid. No one would step into the waters.

"I will be the first," cried out Nachshon of the tribe of Judah. He threw himself into the sea. The tribe of Benjamin followed him.

Only when the Israelites had gone as far as they could and it seemed that the waters would cover their heads did a strong wind come and split the sea so the people could walk on dry ground. The waters formed a wall alongside them.

The chariots still followed, but as soon as the Israelites came out of the sea path, Moses lifted his arm once again. The waters fell over the Egyptians, drowning each one of them.

The Israelites saw that they were safe. On the sandy banks of the sea, they sang a song of praise to God, a song of thanks for all of God's signs and wonders.

The bitter had turned sweet, the fear to joy. The Israelites turned their backs to slavery and began their journey to that desert mountain where they would receive the holy law, the Torah. This law would guide their freedom and give it new meaning.

The Israelites' journey from Egypt and slavery to freedom and Mount Sinai gives us much to remember and retell today. We are ready now to begin the second part of this book, our own Passover journey.

PART TWO

Making
the Israelites'
Journey
Our Own

ABOUT THE SEDER

In the Exodus story, God says, "You are to remember what happens this night and celebrate it throughout the ages."

Jews did and still do celebrate Passover, the night God passed over the houses of the Israelites during the tenth plague, the night Pharaoh said, "Go," the night the Israelites left Egypt in a hurry on the way to freedom and the beginnings of their peoplehood.

We celebrate by remembering and telling stories, by eating certain foods and performing certain rituals. The Rabbis said that in every generation, we should think of ourselves as if *we* were the ones who left Egypt.

We feel as if we are following Moses in the wilderness, eating the flat bread called *matzah* (MA-tzah) instead of the puffed-up leavened bread we eat the rest of the year. We don't know where Moses is leading us, and we are frightened sometimes, but we remind ourselves of the miracles God performed for us in Egypt. We saw the water turn to blood and the land fill with locusts. We saw how the sea parted and gave us a path to walk on. We don't know what lies ahead for us. We feel different, free, at times uncertain, but we are ready to leave our old ways behind and search for new ways to live our lives.

Before Passover, it is traditional to put away the dishes, silverware, pots, and pans used all year and to clean out all the corners of our house of any crumbs of *hametz* (kha-METZ), leavened bread products. We retell and reenact the Exodus story at special dinners on the first two nights of the holiday. All these acts help us relive history in our own homes and in our own lives.

The special dinner called the *Seder* (SAY-der) is the vehicle we use to make the Israelites' journey our journey. The road map we use is a book called a *Haggadah* (ha-ga-DAH). This guide to the Seder gives us words and symbols that help us remember the events of the Exodus and the feelings of the Israelites.

When you sit down at the Seder table, you will not see a dinner all laid out. Not yet. Instead you will see a large plate that holds some unusual foods, foods that are symbols of the Passover story—two kinds of bitter herbs, an apple and nut mixture, a roasted bone, a roasted egg, and fresh greens.

The bitter herbs remind us of the bitterness of slavery. Some people use two kinds at the Seder. One, the horseradish, is bitter from the first bite. The second, the romaine lettuce, tastes sweet at first, but then its taste turns bitter, just as the Israelites' life in Egypt was first sweet and then bitter.

The apple and nut mixture is called *haroset* (kha-RO-set). It looks like the bricks and mortar the Israelites used to build Pharaoh's cities.

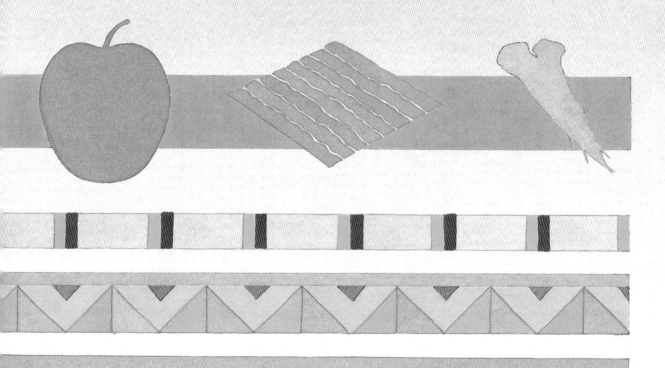

WHY MATZAH?

By eating matzah and not bread on Passover, we remember how the Israelites left Egypt in such a hurry. They did not have time to let their bread dough rise and so ate only the flat cakes called matzot.

The Rabbis tell us something else about matzah, that it is a plain food, the food of slaves and the poor. Bread and other hametz is a puffed-up, fancier food that can be seen as a symbol of pride, greed, and jealousy. On Passover, we try to clean our cupboards of bread and our minds of puffed-upness. Eating the simple bread reminds us to "spring-clean" ourselves, too.

The roasted bone, the *zeroa* (ze-ro-AH), often a lamb shankbone (or a red beet for vegetarian families), is a symbol of the lamb the Israelites roasted and ate quickly on the night they left Egypt.

The roasted egg, *baytzah* (bay-TZAH), represents another offering, the Festival offering given on the three Pilgrimage Festivals in the ancient Temple in Jerusalem. It is also a symbol of new life.

Fresh greens, *karpas* (kar-PAS)—usually parsley, celery, or lettuce—serve as a symbol of springtime and rebirth.

In addition to these foods on the Seder plate, there are three *matzot* (ma-TZOT; plural for matzah) that are covered, a bowl of salt water, wine cups for everyone, as well as another wine cup, a big, beautiful one, for Elijah the Prophet.

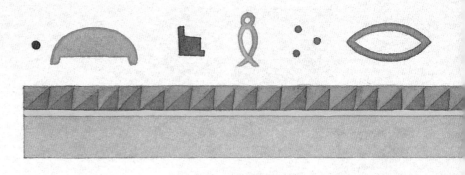

WHY FOUR CUPS OF WINE?

The four cups of wine represent the four promises of freedom God gave to Moses in Exodus 6:6–7. The four promises were that God would bring the Jews out of Egypt, deliver them from slavery, redeem them with an outstretched arm, and make them a nation.

The cup for Elijah is for the prophet we hope will come soon to announce peace among all the peoples of the world.

There will also be place settings for the elaborate meal that comes later, much later, and a Haggadah for each person. Pillows are placed on the chairs because relaxation is an expression of freedom.

In this spirit of rejoicing and freedom, we start the Seder, using the Haggadah as our road map.

There are fourteen signposts on this journey ahead of us. Some instruct us in rituals like washing hands and dipping vegetables in water. Others tell about the story of the Exodus from Egypt and include songs of praise to God.

We are free to meander on this journey, to ask our own questions, add our own comments, to make this retelling our story, too. For the most important thing about the Seder experience is that it makes this ancient event in the history of the Jewish people real to us now.

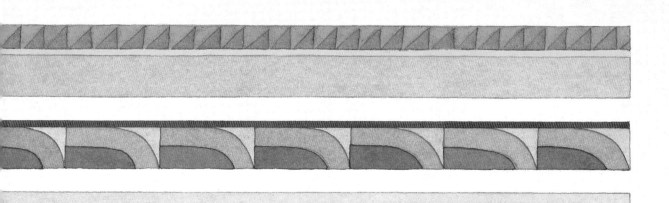

THE FOURTEEN STEPS OF THE SEDER

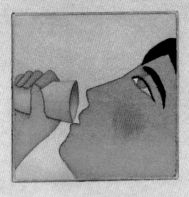

1. KADESH   קַדֵּשׁ

Singing Blessings over the First Cup of Wine

We sing the blessing over the wine or grape juice, lean to the left side, and drink the first cup. The leaning reminds us that in ancient times, only free people could eat the way we do at our Seder, taking our time. Slaves ate hurriedly, standing or squatting, so they could be ready to do their master's work. It seems that everything we do at the Seder is a reminder, even the way we sit and lean.

2. URKHATZ   וּרְחַץ

Washing Hands

Next we wash our hands without saying a blessing. This washing is not the washing of hands before eating, for which there is a blessing. That comes later. This washing is a symbolic one to remind us of the rituals that go back to the days of the Temple in Jerusalem. In those times, our ancestors washed their hands before dipping food into a liquid. Sometimes doing things the way our ancestors did makes us feel closer to them.

3. KARPAS כַּרְפַּס

Dipping a Vegetable in Salt Water

Now we dip a green vegetable, such as parsley or lettuce, into salt water.

The salt water reminds us of the tears of the slaves: their tears when they worked for Pharaoh day after day; their tears when their babies were drowned in the Nile River; their tears when they were beaten by cruel taskmasters.

The greens make us think of springtime, the season of Passover, and of renewed life and hope.

4. YAKHATZ יַחַץ

Breaking the Middle Matzah
and Hiding the Afikoman

Keep a sharp eye out here when the Seder leader takes the middle of the three matzot, breaks it into two pieces, and wraps up the larger one. This piece, the *Afikoman* (a-fee-KO-man), might just disappear when you aren't looking. Watch your parents as they shift in their cushioned chairs or your cousin who goes into the kitchen to check on the soup.

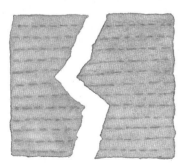

If, somehow, the Afikoman does disappear, you can have the fun of searching for it after the meal. When you find it, there will probably be a surprise for you and maybe a little something for everyone who took part in the search.

5. MAGGID

מַגִּיד

Telling the Passover Story, Including
Asking the Four Questions,
Describing the Four Children
and Drinking the Second Cup of Wine

We've come to the longest part of the Seder. It begins with the youngest children asking the Four Questions.

THE FOUR QUESTIONS

This night is so different from all other nights!

◆ *On other nights, we can eat bread or matzah. But on this night, why do we eat only matzah?*

◆ *On other nights, we eat any kind of vegetable. But on this night, why do we eat bitter herbs?*

◆ *On other nights, we do not have to dip a vegetable even one time. But on this night, why do we dip a vegetable twice?*

◆ *On other nights, we sit anyway we want. But on this night, why do we lean on pillows?*

You may wonder about other things that make this night different. You may wonder why we drink four cups of wine, why we eat a piece of unsweetened matzah for dessert, or why Moses, who was so important in the Passover story, is not mentioned in most Haggadot. Ask *your* questions, too.

The Haggadah gives us some answers to our questions. Why is this night different from all others? Because we were once slaves to Pharaoh and on this night, God took us out of Pharaoh's Egypt. If God had not saved us, all of us and our children and our grandchildren would still be slaves.

So, even if we have read the story of our freedom many times and know it well, we still tell about our Exodus from Egypt. Perhaps talking about our slavery and what it means to be free will help us appreciate our freedom and encourage us to work toward freedom for all peoples.

There are four different places in the Bible that say parents should tell the Passover story to their children.

Because of these four statements, the Rabbis who created the Seder described four children, all different. They understood that since there are different kinds of children, there must be different ways to tell about the Exodus. The important thing is that the story is told so that each child understands it, whether curious and knowledgeable, uninterested and even rebellious, shy and innocent, or unable to ask a question.

THE FOUR CHILDREN

◆ *What does the wise child ask?*

"What are all the laws God has given you about Passover?"

Since the wise child wants to know everything about the holiday, we tell this child all the laws and customs of Passover in great detail.

◆ *What does the wicked child ask?*

"Why do *you* bother with this Seder?"

The wicked child acts like an outsider and does not want to be part of the celebration.

We shock this child, hoping for a change in behavior, by answering: "I celebrate tonight because of what God did for me when I left Egypt. If you had been a slave in Egypt, you would not have been freed with your brothers and sisters."

◆ *What does the innocent child ask?*

"What is this talking all about?"

We explain to this child, "With a mighty hand, God took us out of Egypt, out of slavery."

◆ *What about the child who does not even know how to ask a question?*

We start the discussion for this child by saying, "We celebrate Passover because of what God did for us when we left Egypt."

Some people suggest that there is a little of the Four Children in each one of us, that none of us are all wise, all wicked, all simple, or all unknowing. Each one of us is a mixture. And we ask different kinds of questions as we grow up and change.

Where do you fit in?

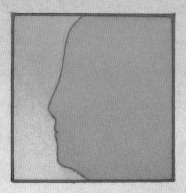

ABOUT MOSES' PLACE IN THE HAGGADAH "WHY DID HE GET LEFT OUT?"

You've seen from reading the story of the Israelites' journey how great a figure Moses was in the Exodus. This may be part of the reason that the Rabbis who put together the traditional Haggadah were careful not to include Moses in the retelling. They did not want people to worship him.

They wanted people to remember that it was God who took the Israelites out of Egypt. Moses was only God's messenger. The Rabbis did not want the people to think that they could free themselves only if they had a strong leader. They could work with God toward freedom in every situation, even without a hero like Moses.

TELLING THE STORY

In this part of the Seder, we talk about the story of the Exodus from Egypt. There are different ways to do this. We can read the retelling in this Haggadah companion or in other books, including excerpts from the book of Exodus in the Bible.

Adults as well as children can take turns around the table talking about the story in their own words. If your family and guests are feeling more adventurous, you could use puppets, mime, charades, dance, or playlets to act out different parts. You could play Moses, your uncle could be Pharaoh, your cousin Pharaoh's daughter. Your little brother won't let you forget that he wants a part, too. A frog in the second plague perhaps? You can make up the words for these plays as you go along.

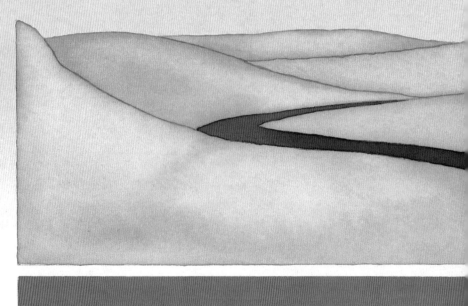

NAMING THE TEN PLAGUES

As we name each plague, we dip a finger or a spoon into our full cup of wine and spill a drop. When the Sea of Reeds closed over Pharaoh's army, the angels in heaven wanted to rejoice and sing songs of praise. But God stopped them, saying, "How can you sing such happy songs when My children are drowning?" By spilling a drop of wine when saying each plague, we remember with sadness the suffering even of our enemies. We empty our cup of joy just a little.

- **Blood**   The water in Egypt turned into blood.
- **Frogs**   And frogs covered the land.
- **Lice**   The dust became lice and the air filled with insects.
- **Beasts**   And wild beasts frightened the Egyptians.
- **Cattle Disease**   The cattle became sick and died.
- **Boils**   And the Egyptians broke out in sores, boils.
- **Hail**   Fiery hail fell from the skies.
- **Locusts**   And swarms of locusts destroyed the crops.
- **Darkness**   The Egyptians experienced darkness in the middle of the day.
- **Death of the Firstborn**   And God passed through the land, killing the Egyptians' firstborn.

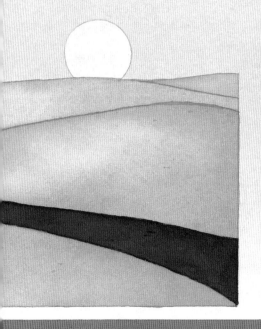

Because we feel thankful for what God did for us in
Egypt, we sing the well known Seder song "*Dayyenu*"
next, and then drink our second cup of wine.

If God had just taken us out of Egypt,
   Dayyenu. It would have been enough.
If God had just given us the Sabbath,
   Dayyenu. It would have been enough.
If God had just given us the Torah,
   Dayyenu. It would have been enough.
But God took us out of Egypt *and*
   punished the Egyptians *and*
   divided the sea for us *and*
   led us across on dry land *and*
   cared for us for forty years in the desert *and*
   fed us manna *and*
   gave us the Sabbath *and*
   brought us to Mount Sinai *and*
   gave us the Torah *and*
   led us to the land of Israel *and*
   built the Temple for us.

   Dayyenu.

   דַּיֵּנוּ

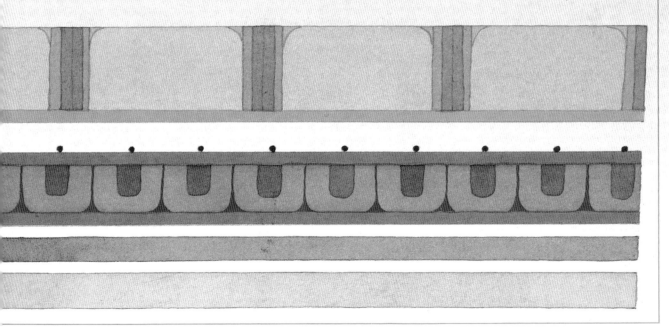

CUSTOMS FROM OTHER LANDS FOR THE TELLING

Adapted from a Sephardic custom

Someone goes out of the room and knocks on the door.

"Who's there?" you ask.

"A Jew," he or she answers.

"Where are you from?"

"Egypt."

"What did you do there?"

"I was a slave."

"Where are you going?"

"I don't know. I'm following Moses."

"What are you carrying?"

"I'm carrying matzah because I didn't have time to make bread."

"How long did it take you to get here?"

"Forty years."

And so the questions go back and forth and make the Exodus seem more real.

From an ancient Baghdad custom

The Seder leader asks the children questions as if they were the Israelites leaving Egypt.

"If you were leaving Egypt three thousand years ago, how would you get ready for the journey? What would you take? How would you feel?"

From an Oriental custom

You can pretend you are an Israelite about to walk out of Egypt. You could drape a sheet around you or wear a bathrobe. Put matzah on your left shoulder, sandals on your feet, and hold on to a walking stick. Then march around the table, into other rooms, even outside in the street to relive the Exodus.

After this "telling" part of the Haggadah, we do a few more rituals that prepare us to eat our meal and also remind us of the slavery and freedom we have just talked about.

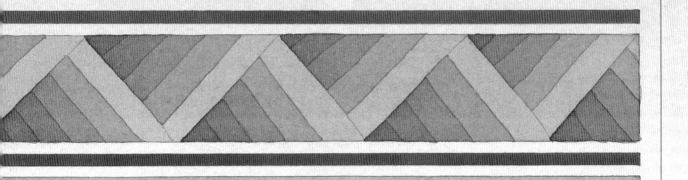

6. RAKHTZAH רָחְצָה

Washing the Hands Before the Meal

We wash our hands and say the blessing in preparation for the meal.

7. MOTZEE MATZAH מוֹצִיא מַצָּה

Saying the Blessings for Matzah

We say blessings over the matzah. One is a blesssing that is said all year for bread and one is said especially for matzah.

8. MAROR מָרוֹר

Tasting the Bitter Herbs and
Dipping Them in Haroset

For the second time at the Seder, we dip. This time we dip *maror* (ma-ROAR), bitter herbs, into haroset, the sweet apple-and-nut mixture.

The Haggadah has us use our senses to experience slavery; it doesn't rely only on words to help us relive our ancestors' journey. Tasting the bitterness of maror is like tasting a little of the bitterness of slavery. Even smelling the maror may make your eyes water and your nose run. Looking at the reddish brown color of the haroset is like looking at the mortar and bricks our ancestors used to make buildings for Pharaoh. Tasting again, this time of the haroset, gives us a little surprise, because it is sweet and leaves our senses with a reminder of the hope of freedom.

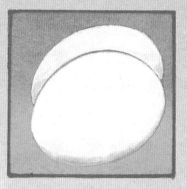

WHY HARD-BOILED EGGS?

Many families serve hard-boiled eggs dipped in salt water to start the meal. Some say the eggs represent spring and new life. Others say this was a custom in Roman times and that eggs were served at Seder meals two thousand years ago. Some say the egg reminds us of the sacrifices at the Temple service in Jerusalem and of the destruction of the Temple.

9. KOREKH   כּוֹרֵךְ

Eating a Matzah and Bitter Herb Sandwich

A famous sage of long ago, named Hillel, ate matzah and bitter herbs together. When you eat this Hillel sandwich, think of tasting freedom and slavery together and of how the matzah of the slave became the matzah of the free. Think of the bitterness and the joy of the Passover story.

10. SHULKHAN OREKH   שֻׁלְחָן עוֹרֵךְ

Enjoying the Festival Meal

Now we are at the part of the Seder everyone has been eager for, the meal. Enough of the little teasers of parsley and matzah and crushed nuts, apples, and wine; enough of history and rituals, questions and answers.

Our stomachs are rumbling, and we all want to sink our teeth into Mom's matzah balls and chicken soup, Uncle Sol's brisket of beef and sweet carrot stew, and Aunt Ida's sponge cake. Take time to enjoy this part of the Seder, and when you are full and rested, we will talk and sing and remember some more.

WHY THE AFIKOMAN?

Some people say that the Rabbis put this Afikoman search into the Seder just to keep the children awake through all the songs and stories. The Rabbis knew what they were doing, because few children can sleep when they know there will be a treasure hunt after dinner, the treasure being a piece of matzah and a prize.

In Temple times, the Passover sacrifice, the roasted lamb, was eaten at the end of the meal. We substitute this small piece of matzah for the lamb as the very last bit of food we eat at the Seder.

11. TZAFUN   צָפוּן

Finding and Eating the Afikoman

It's time to hunt for the Afikoman, that half of the middle matzah that was wrapped in a napkin and hidden hours ago. When you play this game with the Afikoman, think for a minute of the slaves then, and poor people now, who have so little to eat that they often put some of their food away to save for later, for a time when they may have nothing to eat.

Some families have a different way to play hide-and-seek with the Afikoman. In these homes it is the children, instead of the Seder leader, who steal the Afikoman and hide it. Either way, when the meal is over, they often refuse to give it back. This can get a spirited bargaining session going with the Seder leader for a better prize—since the Seder cannot continue until the Afikoman is found and a small piece eaten by everyone at the table.

12. BAREKH בָּרֵךְ

Singing the Blessings After the Meal, Drinking the Third Cup of Wine, and Opening the Door for the Prophet Elijah

Once again we all settle in our chairs around the Seder table, the children excited about their search and surprises, the adults relaxed after their tea and coffee and chance to chat with one another. Feeling satisfied, we sing the blessings that thank God for our food and company, our holy laws, and our freedom, and we drink the third cup of wine.

It is at this point in the Seder that many people remember other times in our history when we were slaves. Some interpret the Hebrew word for Egypt, *Mitzrayim,* to mean "straits" or "narrow place," a place in which we were confined. There have been other Egypts, other narrow places, and other Pharaohs in our long history.

THE WARSAW GHETTO: A "NARROW PLACE"

A ghetto was a part of a city in which Jews were required to live by law. Starting in the 1500s in many cities in Europe, Jews were forced to leave their homes and move into cramped quarters in these designated areas. Often other restrictions would be placed on them, such as curfews and wearing special badges that labeled them as Jews.

Just before Passover 1943, the Jews of Warsaw, Poland, prepared defenses against the Nazi Germans, who planned to storm the ghetto. Thousands of civilians, led by the Jewish Fighting Organization and the Jewish Military Association, barricaded the entrances to their courtyards and homes with upturned wagons and heavy pieces of furniture. They placed sandbags on windowsills to lean on during the shooting.

Stashes of hand grenades, bombs, rifles, food—and poison tablets to be taken in case of capture—were stored in the attics, apartments, cellars, and secret underground bunkers of the ghetto. The fly prepared to battle the elephant.

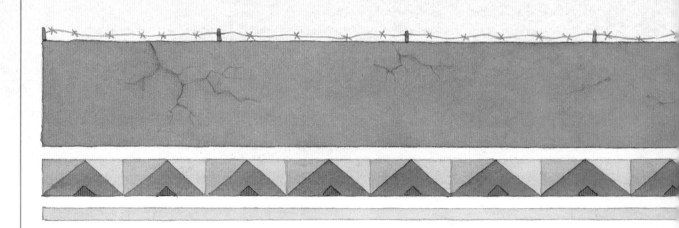

Early on the morning of April 19, the day of the first Seder, more than two thousand Ukrainian and German soldiers, followed by heavy trucks, ambulances, a field kitchen, armored tanks, and field telephones, entered the ghetto. When the German column neared Nalewki and Gensia streets, it was greeted by a shower of bombs, bullets, and hand grenades. The surprised Nazis fled in a state of panic. The ghetto was fighting!

That night after the Germans withdrew their forces, the Jews of the Warsaw Ghetto sat down in their bunkers to celebrate the Seder with feelings of pride and apprehension. Outside, their blue-and-white banners still flew in the streets.

It took the Nazis some forty days to subdue and destroy the Warsaw Ghetto, longer than it had taken them to conquer the countries of Poland or France.

If guests at your Seder lived through the Holocaust, those years of Nazi Germany's war against the Jews and other peoples, ask them if they want to add their personal story to this evening's discussions. Perhaps some of your Seder guests have moved here from the Soviet Union. They, too, have a story to tell of their "narrow place." And there are stories about the building of Israel, where many people escaping narrow places found a new home, a refuge from persecution.

By telling these stories, we remember the bitterness and joy of the two worlds, slavery and freedom. We remember freedom even in the darkest times and slavery even in the times of light.

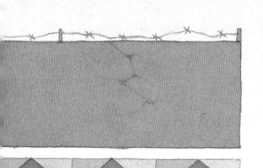

FILLING ELIJAH'S CUP

One way to fill Elijah's cup is to pass it from person to person at the table. Each person pours a little wine into this special cup to show that we must all work together to bring about the days of peace.

ELIJAH'S CUP—SYMBOL OF HOPE

The Bible tells us that Elijah the Prophet never died but was lifted to heaven in a fiery chariot within a great whirlwind. Many stories through the ages tell of Elijah's reappearance on earth, dressed in different disguises, to help those in need, to guide and to teach.

Elijah also has a role in bringing about the time of the Messiah, the days of peace. Elijah will announce these days, settle all quarrels, and establish harmony in the world. At the sound of his trumpet, the primal light that shone before the creation will fill the world, and evil will be banished forever.

Because Jews eagerly await the time of peace, they are always looking for Elijah, hoping he will come this year, perhaps at this very Seder.

In honor of Elijah, we place a large and beautiful wine cup on the Seder table and invite him in by opening the door so he can drink from his cup. Some children check and say they do see less wine in the cup. Do you?

When you open the door for the great prophet, you may feel a shiver of excitement, of anticipation. You may hope that this year will be different, a time of peace in the world. Are you ready to do your part? To share in the work of repairing the world? To meet Elijah halfway?

13. HALLEL   הַלֵּל

Singing Psalms of Praise and
Drinking the Fourth Cup of Wine

Before we end the Seder, we sing psalms praising God, who took us from slavery to freedom, from sadness to joy, from darkness to great light. Then we drink the fourth and last cup of wine.

14. NIRTZAH   נִרְצָה

Completing the Seder with Traditional Songs

Feeling a mixture of tiredness and excitement, we end the Seder with songs. While you are singing, think of our journey tonight.

Looking at the Seder table, we see the familiar matzah and salt water, roasted egg, and Elijah's cup. We see the bitterness of our ancestors' lives and the hope they still carried within them. We see that a symbol of slavery, matzah, can also be a symbol of freedom. And we carry these symbols and thoughts into our own lives as reminders of our history, our ups and downs, our sorrows and joys, and above all our faith and longing for a sweet and peaceful future.

This song, sung every year at the Seder, expresses that longing—and our hope—for peace:

Next year in Jerusalem!
Next year in a Jerusalem at peace!
לַשָׁנָה הַבָּאָה בִּירוּשָׁלָיִם

ONE LITTLE GOAT   חַד גַּדְיָא

This Passover favorite tells the story of a little goat bought for two coins, two *zuzim*. It is eaten by a cat that is bitten by a dog that is beaten by a stick that is burned by a fire that is quenched by water that is drunk by an ox that is slaughtered by a butcher who is called for by the Angel of Death, who is killed by the Holy One. The singing of this song traditionally ends the Seder until next year.

Some suggest that the one little goat, *khad gadya,* stands for the Jewish people, and that the two zuzim represent Moses and Aaron, who led the Jews out of Egypt with God's help. The remaining characters in the song stand for different enemies of the Jewish people, all of whom were destroyed.

One little goat, one little goat,
That my father bought for two *zuzim*,
One little goat, one little goat.

Then came the cat that ate the goat
That my father bought for two *zuzim*,
One little goat, one little goat.

Then came a dog that bit the cat
That ate the goat
That my father bought for two *zuzim*,
One little goat, one little goat. . . .

Then came the Holy One and killed the Angel of Death
Who called for the butcher
Who slaughtered the ox
That drank the water
That put out the fire
That burned the stick
That beat the dog
That bit the cat
That ate the goat
That my father bought for two *zuzim*,
One little goat, one little goat.
Khad gadya, khad gadya.

Until next year!

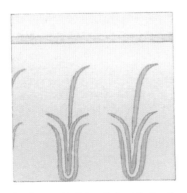

NOTES ON SOURCES

The first part of this Seder companion, "The Israelites' Journey: The Story of the Exodus," is based on the Jewish Publication Society's translation of the book of Exodus. Intermingled throughout the retelling are stories from Midrash.

The word *midrash* means "to search out, to expound." A midrash is a story that explains or elaborates on a passage in the Bible. The stories from Midrash added to the Exodus story here were told by Rabbis who lived about 200–500 C.E. I found them in sources such as the *Babylonian Talmud,* a sacred text compiled by the Rabbis themselves that expounds on the Torah, and *The Legends of the Jews* by the noted twentieth-century Bible scholar Louis Ginzberg.

The story of three-year-old Moses, for instance, who reaches for a piece of coal, is a story from Midrash, as is the story of Pharaoh wandering through the streets of Goshen looking for Moses' house. In this way, this particular retelling of the Exodus adds the richness and depth of rabbinic commentary about the characters and events of the Exodus to the biblical story.

In writing the second part of this Seder companion, I drew on many versions of the Haggadah and on source books to present and explain the steps and customs of the Seder. I also tried to use language that is nonsexist.

The basic part of the traditional Haggadah is at least a thousand years old. However, the Haggadah and the Seder to which it is a guide have undergone changes and additions over the years, reflecting the history of the times and the people who participate.

The Seder and the Haggadah are part of a process of making this holiday one's own. There are many different family customs and over three thousand editions of the Haggadah now available to choose from. One takes from here and there to add to the Seder to make the celebration as meaningful and personal as possible.

The section on the Warsaw Ghetto is based on the books *The Jews of Warsaw* by Yisrael Gutman and *They Fought Back* by Yuri Suhl.

The four different places in the Bible that say parents should tell the Passover story to their children are Exodus 12:26, 13:8, 13:14, and Deuteronomy 6:20.

GLOSSARY

Afikoman (a-fee-KO-man) is the broken piece of the middle matzah, which is wrapped up, hidden, and later searched for by the children. A piece of the Afikoman is eaten at the end of the Seder meal.

Baytzah (bay-TZAH) is the roasted egg on the Seder plate, which represents the festival offering in the ancient Temple. It is also a symbol of springtime.

B.C.E. stands for Before the Common Era, used to mark the years before the birth of Jesus. **C.E.** stands for Common Era.

Elijah (e-LI-jah) was a prophet in Israel in the ninth century B.C.E. who, after zealously fighting to preserve the worship of the One God, ascended to heaven in a fiery chariot. Numerous stories throughout the ages tell of his reappearances on earth to help those in need.

Exodus (EK-se-des) refers to the departure of the Israelites from Egypt, which archaeological research designates as the thirteenth century B.C.E. Exodus is also the second book of the Five Books of Moses and contains an account of this departure.

Haggadah (ha-ga-DAH) is the book that serves as a guide to conducting the Seder. It explains the symbols on the Seder table and tells the story of the Exodus of the Israelites from Egypt. The story is embellished with commentary, song, and praises.

Haggadot (ha-ga-DOT) is plural for Haggadah.

Hametz (kha-METZ) is any food not kosher for Passover, such as leavened bread products, cereals, and grains—especially wheat, barley, spelt, oats, and rye. Ashkenazic Jews (of Eastern European origin) include rice, millet, corn, and legumes.

Haroset (kha-RO-set) is a mixture, most often of apples, nuts, wine, and cinnamon, that reminds Seder participants of the bricks and mortar the Israelites used to build Pharaoh's cities.

Karpas (kar-PAS) is the fresh greens on the Seder plate, which are a symbol of springtime and rebirth.

Kosher (KO-sher) refers to food and eating utensils that are ritually permitted according to Jewish law.

Manna (MAN-a) was the special food God gave the Israelites while they wandered in the desert after the Exodus from Egypt.

Maror (ma-ROAR) is a bitter herb, such as horseradish, which symbolizes the bitter life of the Israelite slaves under Pharaoh.

Matzah (MA-tzah) is the flat, unleavened bread the Israelites ate while they were slaves in Egypt and on the night they fled from slavery.

Matzot (ma-TZOT) is plural for matzah.

Messiah (me-SI-ah) literally meaning "anointed one," is the title applied to the descendant of King David who will rule over Israel in the days of peace, the golden age.

Mount Sinai (Mount SI-nai) is a mountain in the Sinai Desert. Its exact location is unknown. It was on this mountain that Moses received the Ten Commandments after the Exodus from Egypt.

Passover (PASS-o-ver) is the eight-day festival commemorating the Exodus from Egypt and freedom from slavery. It is also called the Spring Festival or the Festival of Unleavened Bread.

Pharaoh (FAIR-o) was the title of the ancient Egyptian king.

The Pilgrimage Festivals are the three holidays on which a pilgrimage to the ancient Temple in Jerusalem is prescribed by the Torah. They are Passover, Shavuot, and Sukkot.

Sedarim (si-dah-REEM) is plural for Seder.

Seder (SAY-der) refers to the special dinner held on the first two nights of Passover. The word means "order" and specifically refers to the order

of the ceremony on those two nights. Reform Jews and Jews in Israel have only one Seder.

Torah (toe-RAH) refers to the Five Books of Moses. It can also mean the entire body of Jewish law. The literal meaning of Torah is "teaching."

Zeroa (ze-ro-AH) is the roasted shank bone on the Seder plate, which is a symbol of the lamb the Israelites roasted and ate on the night they left Egypt.

ABOUT
THE AUTHOR
AND
ILLUSTRATOR

BARBARA DIAMOND GOLDIN says, "While I was growing up, Passover was one of my favorite holidays. My mother cleaned and cooked for days beforehand; my two younger brothers and I helped her. We carried boxes of holiday dishes upstairs from the basement, then washed and dried them. We tied rope around the handles of cupboards filled with the year-round dishes. By the time we were finished, everything in the kitchen was either different, new, or covered up.

"The Sedarim at our house were lively. We all joked about Mom's matzah balls and the amount of food she put on the table. Finding the Afikoman was a bigger and bigger challenge every year, and we never knew who was going to walk through the door when we opened it for Elijah. One year it was a cat, and another year, my father's friend Teddy.

"When my grandfather, and later my father, led the Seder, we all read and sang our way through the whole Haggadah. Though I didn't understand every part, I loved performing the rituals, like dipping the wine out of my cup for the ten plagues and making a Hillel sandwich of horseradish and matzah. (We always 'cheated' by adding gobs of haroset to sweeten the taste.)

"Passover continues to be an important holiday to me now. Every year, I learn more about the traditions and learn new ways to add meaning to the Sedarim. For several years, I've participated in Sedarim at my friends Rabbi Daniel and Hanna Tiferet Siegel's house. During the Seder, like the Yemenites, we nibble on romaine lettuce leaves that cover the entire table. I like the green and springlike look the lettuce brings to the Seder table.

"Over the past few years, I have found that eating different foods, performing different rituals, and changing my habits on Passover make it clearer and clearer to me how ingrained I have become in old routines and patterns. I find that the changes Passover brings encourage looking at life and the world a bit differently—all year long."

Barbara Diamond Goldin is the author of *Just Enough Is Plenty,* illustrated by Seymour Chwast and winner of the National Jewish Book Award, and *Cakes and Miracles,* illustrated by Erika Weihs and winner of the Association of Jewish Libraries Award (both Viking and Puffin).

NEIL WALDMAN shares two Passover memories: "As a young child in the Bronx, I always celebrated Passover at my grandparents' apartment. The memories of those Sedarim are stored in my mind like precious paintings. The living room is bathed in a soft, golden light. Cousins, aunts, uncles, and friends are snugly seated around a huge table. The tablecloth is shining white, though I can't see much of it, as my eyes are just above tabletop level. I gaze across a sea of sparkling crystal, china, and silver to the face of my beloved Grandpa Meyer. He clears his throat and opens his Haggadah, and I await the sound of his gravelly voice.

"The Seder at Kibbutz Neve Ur in Israel was a completely different experience. In the dining hall of the kibbutz, five hundred people loudly read from our agrarian socialist Haggadah. The seriousness of the occasion was soon drowned in wine, as we emptied four very full glasses. Then we ate and began to sing . . . and sing . . . and sing. The families of our kibbutz came from forty different nations, and someone got the idea that each nation should be represented by a Passover song in that native tongue. By the time we finished singing, it was four in the morning."

Neil Waldman has illustrated more than fifteen books, including *The Sea Lion* by Ken Kesey (Viking). He lives in Westchester, New York.